WITHDRAWN
NDSU

3 00/NO + 60 PH
EN

AN IRISH ALBUM

ROBIN SKELTON

An Irish Album

THE DOLMEN PRESS

233523

Set in Plantin type and printed and published in the
Republic of Ireland at The Dolmen Press Limited, 8 Herbert Place, Dublin 2.

Distributed outside Ireland, except in the U.S.A. and Canada
by Oxford University Press
and in the U.S.A. and Canada by Dufour Editions Inc.,
Chester Springs, Pennsylvania 19425.
1969

PR
6037
K39
I64

© *1969: Robin Skelton*

FOR LIAM

CONTENTS

FOR DUBLIN WITH LOVE

To fall in love with Ireland
is to court
a ghost with the smile of a mother,
the eyes of a girl
giddy with singing,
and the white skin of a clerk
intent with brush
on the cracking page of a Missal.

I have been betrayed
into this liaison
by the formidable Uncles,
cavern-toned,
stamping the boards of their stage,
announcing heroes,
pouring me through the city
on bell-tongued tides.

Hunted, I cannot escape her,
no more than Joyce
recalling the curve of her buttock
in Zurich streets
and mouthing his lover's babble,
inventing words
to trouble the wry-necked clerics
above their books.

No one can ever escape her
once her head
has turned in the turning sunlight,

gold and grey
as changing silks of the curtain
dropped across
the sun from a cloud of mourning
above the sea.

No one resembles her. No one.
Byzantium's been
outclassed by her streetgirl dance,
and Ilium veiled
in the dignity of her suffering,
Rome reduced
to dust by her narrow insistence,
her generous smile.

I have been trapped,
and I tangle traditional robes
in postures of adoration,
skin my fingers
on strings that snap like a mousetrap
or hang slack
on a harp that abuses my eardrums
and cricks my neck.

Nothing as funny has happened
to please her for years,
not since George Moore learned the Gaelic
and tried to skip
to the sound of an unstrung fidil
in County Mayo;
or that beanpole Anglo-Irishman
launched his ship

on a tide of prosaic pretensions,
a hooker of Galway
rhyming the prices of fish;
or Yeats, in a fury
of scholarly misdirection,
made Blake an O'Neill,
and sat Urizen down in Kiltartan
to spell a Rann.

But laughter has never perturbed her.
Hot-eyed fools,
innocent in their passion
and transformed
by urgent ridiculous loyalties,
have her forgiveness;
even the maddened sobrieties
of the learned

can be excused, then forgotten,
while steel-eyed censors
raging with purity,
burning the *News of the World*,
and watchful for mention of underwear,
are admitted
equally into the company
of Saints and Scholars.

Indiscriminate Ireland,
Ireland crazed
by the hearts affections,
the pure zest of the mind,
the long dance of the tongue,

the remembered suffering,
Ireland innocent, vivid,
wondering, bland,
troubles me like the drink.

The formidable Uncles
brought me into her house,
and in sonorous tones
said something inappropriate;
on the wall
was a photograph of Maud Gonne
with a boss-eyed hound,

and a purple Paul Henry landscape.
I looked. I listened.
A voice rose out of an inkwell
and talked of graves.
A bottle of Inisfree Water
whispered Thalatta,
and someone in snot-green silk
took a flag and waved

to the tenor elongating syllables
till they festooned the
room with a seaweed of ribbons
upon which bells
tolled Angelus,
and seven Sisters of Mercy
told seven tales of Saint Patrick
to seven gulls

come in from Lord Nelson's shoulder.
I looked. I listened.
A man in an ulster
ate oranges from a plate
entirely covered in shamrock,
spitting the golden
pips in a rage of humility
at his fate.

And a black-bearded printer
piled sugarlumps into a dolmen
from which sweetness dropped,
drip by drip, on the upturned mouths
of sixteen poets, seven playwrights,
and forty-five scholars
engaged in outlining the final,
the ultimate truth

about Synge, about Yeats, about Swift,
about Tara, commenting
in between drips
on the terrible state of the nation.
I looked and I listened.
And then one remarkable Uncle
led me outback to the stars
that filled the spaces

between the grey decorous squares,
and I heard a singing.
The words were no matter;

they came clear and keen
as a flute across lake water,
as if the mountains
around the city
hunched to a secret tune

that no one could hear but the once.
I heard it, listened
to something still and chill
from the riot heart;
a blackbird under a hedgerow
might have known it,
or a curlew high on the moorland;
wilder than art,

and stranger than music,
it wandered like a woman
wandering, remote with love,
an unending garden,
impersonal in her possessing.
It soared, it fluttered,
delicate, vibrant, absurd
as the heart is absurd

always when touched or abandoned.
It was that moment
Ireland turned her head
and I caught the gleam,
stood there, ridiculous,
clumsy with alien language,
dropping my half eaten syllables
on the stones,

and wiping my mouth with a sleeve
that tasted of Guinness,
and feeling the wind round my heart.
Remote, absurd,
that sweetness lingered and lingers.
Back from exile,
I have made this poem
that the ghost may return.

FIRST ENCOUNTER

In Homage to Robert Flaherty

The first film that I saw
  was *Man of Aran*.
Five years old, I sat in the
  dark and stared
at the relentless seas,
  the raking stones,
the coracles. They'd thought it
  was *Treasure Island*

and were disappointed for me.
  The Atlantic
broke through the watching rows
  of the holy room,
drowning, battering.
  The next week
it was Long John Silver,
  pieces-of-eight, and Pew

ancient and blind as Raftery!
  But I carried
Aran there in my head,
  and palm-fronds shook
to the gasp of breakers;
  hunched up in the dark
of everywhere, my tensed hands
  gripped at rock,

exultant, secret.
    Though the holiday sands
were printed upon the screen
    with swords and spades
and parrotting adventurers,
    behind
their dwarf games walked the
    giant of the wind

I knew ahead of me.
    The murdering treasure
shone like candy.
    Swords and ships and guns
faded against the rock.
    I was a rock.
Blindly I walked out,
    Aran, to the sun.

SUIBHNE IN THE FOREST

After the Irish

Huge-headed oak,
you are tall, tall.
Small hazel, pick
me your secret nuts.

Alder, friendly one,
gleam, shine;
you bar no gap
with a toothed thorn.

Blackthorn, dark one,
provide sloes;
watercress, brim
the blackbirds' pools.

Small one, pathway
loiterer, green
leaved berry, give me
your specked crimson.

Apple tree, let me
shake you strongly.
Rowan, drop me
your bright blossom.

Briar, relent.
Your hooks have fed

content till you
are filled with blood.

Church Yew, calm
me with grave talk.
Ivy, bring dream
through the dark wood.

Hollybush, bar me
from winter winds.
Ash, be a spear
in my fearful hand.

Birch, oh blessed
birchtree, sing
proudly the tangle
of the wind.

WREN BOYS

Dead bird and holly branch; red berry
red as the smear on the small beak;
green leaves glossy as brown feathers
filling with winter; shrill words
ragged as breeches; Christ, betrayed
by the smallest children of wild air,

remembered for pennies the day stones
knocked the first martyr to slumped meat:
fingers thin as the wren bones
clutch sticks, and hoarse throats
chant for charity as a chill
mist creeps from the near hills,

recalling martyrs: cold men
shivering the danks of a good death
by gun or hunger; young men
drunk on the holy kiss of wraiths,
the high sweet songs; dark men, abandoned
into the furious needs of saints,

narrowed and watchful. Smoke drifts
from chimneys, settles. Christmas tolled
that lolling droleen to its branch,
and gave the cause to boast its fall.
Sticks lift and clack. From crouching hills
the ancient sure miasma rolls.

SONG AT TWILIGHT

Backside strapped
and ear sermoned,
I heard blackbirds
in half light
on my way prepwards;
great chestnuts
cluttered with candles
shook leaves.

Schoolboy faces
and holy fathers
recall that bitter
keen delight
in Dublin suburbs;
subdued files
trooping past railings
send waves

roaring through thirty
years of hearing
different blackbirds,
darker texts,
to flood chestnuts,
light candles,
echo the lonely
blessing asked.

HER BEAUTY

After the 18*th Century Irish*

She is the blackberry's
whitest flower,
the raspberry cane's
most delicate petal,
the queen of all simples
in the herbal
smoothing beauty
on aching eyes.

She is the pulse
my veins wander,
my secret creature,
my apple blossom
flared like a miracle
time of summer
in the middle
of winter snows.

THE TWO WINTERS
After the Irish

1. *Finn's Message*

I bring news:
the stag bells;
winter drenches;
the summer dies.

The wind is high,
the sun low
and its path short.
There are strong tides.

Bracken is red,
all patterning lost;
barnacle geese
cry overhead.

Cold grips the wings
of the hunched birds.
Ice is in season.
Hear my news.

2. *Oisin's Lament*

Once my hair was
curled and yellow;
now my head is
a grey stubble.

I would rather
be raven locked
than specked grey
by this dry frost.

I cannot make love
for the women sneer.
Spring is a winter
of grey hair.

THE OLD WOMAN OF BEARE
After the Irish

Yellowed by age,
I'm ebbing fast,
and weep for the way
that Death makes haste.

Though once each dress
made the young men stare,
now I'm "that dirty
old bitch of Beare".

These days it's money
that makes the man;
we spat on pennies
when I was young.

We cheered the horses
and chariot races—
God bless the dead
Kings for their pleasures!

We went with farmers
among the corn;
they loved us well
and they held their tongues.

These days they're quicker
to ask and get,
but they do damn little
and boast a lot,

while my good body
is old and sick—
Christ in Your Mercy
take me quick!

Girls in their heyday
are gay and bold,
but I am destroyed
to have got so old.

My arms are bony
and stiff and thin
that once curved soft
round the necks of Kings.

There's nothing to
whisper any more,
and no one gasps
at my withered hair.

I don't give a damn
what I put on my head,
though once I was
careful enough and proud.

But I envy no one
—except that field,
for while I wither
its hair turns gold,

and Drumhain's cloak
when it changes green
for snows of ermine
looks just as fine,

while the Stone of the Kings
and Renan's Hall,
though storm-beaten,
don't age at all.

The tides are rising;
the winter's near;
there's never a hope
of visitors.

The young men are off
in their boats by the reeds,
and will sleep deep
in their makeshift beds,

but my days of sailing
are long since done,
and all my talent
for love is gone,

and now, however
warm the days,
I need my cloak
and I feel my age.

My summer's over,
my autumn's past,
and all I've left
is a bitter frost.

I've had my fun,
jumped over the wall;
would virtue have made
any difference at all?

I've had my fill
of those Royal jags;
now I sip thin whey
with the other hags.

Thin whey! No ale!
May all I suffer
seem God's good will
not cause for anger.

One eye is failing;
the other's blind;
I'm bankrupt both
of my sight and land.

We flood, then ebb:
what the high tide sends
the ebb-tide sucks
from your still wet hands.

Ebb follows flood!
Time after time
I've seen it happen.
I know the signs.

That island is blessed,
for its flood returns.
I ebb without hope
for my emptying arms.

THE OLD ONE

Old Woman, though you are old,
rubbing your cold fingers
thick as potatoes round
the young husband you've held,
it is the old ones know
the trick of it. I sing
a warm practised mouth
and breasts of dried leather.

Old Woman, when you fall,
knowing all, you squander
a scholar body, wise
in which to disguise, which tell:
it is the old ones know
the lie of it. I toast
an old heart-gladdening coach
easing the love-learner.

Old Woman, past your best,
proud of your list of lovers,
you got but little rest,
boasting of the nights
and of dawns breaking, know
I cannot but revere
the stamina of a hulk
still tight after such weathers.

Old Woman, forgive me if
old is a rough answer
to those hard brown teeth
still biting more youth off
the fallen world. You know
the sweetening bruise. I swear
it's that salt on the meat
makes my mouth sweat with hunger.

And what of the young girls?
There's none calls to her lover
cleanly as a bird
but when hard times befall
has nothing of what you know,
who bore them all. The limber
cruelty of the young
will never win me over

unless yourself provides,
Old Woman, who remember
more sauce to the dish
than any, and brush past
brute morals, wise to know
love burlier, and a weathered
beam outlasting any
however sweet-pithed other.

THE FEAST OF SAINT BRIGID

After the 10*th Century Irish*

I'd like the men of Heaven
in my own cabin
with barrels and barrels of ale
there for the drinking.

I'd like to welcome the famous
three sweet Marys
and people from every corner
of Paradise.

I'd want them all to be singing
at their drinking,
and Jesus too to be there
and celebrating.

I'd have a great sea of beer
for my King and Saviour
and watch the whole Family drinking
for ever and ever.

WHO WEEPS FOR DEDALUS

I

Silence, Exile, Cunning. A sham boast,
his long tongue clicking like a two-hinged door
to let her grey streets in, his fingers full
upon her: and what cunning can adore
so openly, so inwardly? The bite
of inwit was their wedding flea each night.

Nor he alone but others, ruined, spoiled,
beggared, crazed, poxed. What a wench is this
can be supremely nymph, colleen, or mott,
nun, vestal, courtesan, aunt, mother, miss,
or mistress; any shift is one she'll take
to twist the silence through a new heartbreak.

Four husbands she has had among the rest;
some say at one time, and some say one by one.
Monastery and Castle roofed in two;
a third put up his money at an Inn
as gunfire knocked the streets, while number four
leaned, and leans yet, against the cunning bar,

disreputably still, mind on a horse,
eyes bright with accidie. It's here she'll stay
the world out now. All other beds are cold;
her mouth is thirsty, and her eyes, as grey
as any fabled queen's or murdered stone,
mock history for the centuries it has done.

II

She weeps for Dedalus. She lifts
head high in weeds by greenest of canals,
her handmaids. Drowned as anyone is drowned,
they say he sleeps upon his fathered bed
fathoms under foam, and all the saints
may from their Paulpits practice on the brass.

Who would not weep for Dedalus? She mourns
innumerably, and even if no words
loom darkly in the dead glass of his hand,
she yet, the kissed and cuddler of the dead
from Oisin on, enfolds him; still he lives
and nectar pure with oozy licks he laves

while curates pull the engine. Unfrocked priest,
descutcheoned duke, and bankrupt banker, host
to all the past he isn't, here his head
is meddled on the ribbon that she's led
all this bull in by, careless if she loose
more myths to mouth, call chaos into place

as long as ebbflows, tidesturn, while timends
with towels on and no more births resound.

III

Allwise the elegiac night it is;
each eve's All Hollows to the goats that work
this urnshent city of so moony dead;
hear in the gordian straits a fidil plies
its harmonies while on Saint Starving's Groin
the midnote corpses wrestle : illstars know
allwise the elegiac night it is.

Eelwoes the ruining river runes and keens;
the mummeries gripe togather weir the stops
acurse the groaned canaille to Bigot's Treat
wring out like hawsers heaves; he leans, she liens
lo on the purrypat, recurling all
posed wards and locks; though hewman dies may end
eelwoes the ruining river runes and keens.

Wholewars and holeways we drown under words,
the beg or smile, the dune or the undawn;
though impures foul and notions louse their why
and ovary servilization brakes lake bards
whose patterns mute the gael, and, though betried
by her again, agone in mournlilt years
wholewars and holeways we drown under words.

SUIBHNE REDIVIVUS

Constructing my poem
like a pint of porter,
a drop too lively, a drop sour
to freshen, then flatten
and make all creamy,
more of a curate than a seer
in this snug study,
the brass banded
pumps of metaphor well worn
by the clutching fingers,
the calendar
numbered to death by the black phone,
here I am, working,
smoke and chatter
blinding as always, the hard stuff
heady as ever,
the Powers golden,
the Harp just lucid and wild enough,
when who comes in
but the ghost of Suibhne
rattling the keys to his new Ford,
freshly befeathered.
"To hell with trees.
It's maybe a great yolk for a bird,
but never a man",
he says, "I'm trying
Dublin City, the new attraction!
A little mott

in O'Connell Street
said there was plenty of conversation
the way I'd want it.
Being a poet
myself, I'm in chase of a few writers
quick with the rhyme
for a good drink,
but everywhere they are saying '*Jazus,
we've none of that.
Its' all the pictures
and Telefis Eireann now for them,
and off to America
every minute
reciting to those Hollywood women.
The old ones are dead.
You remember Mangan?
There was a man with a fine thought!
And Yeats now, Yeats
was a class of man
you wouldn't be wrong to call a poet.
But your man now
is a different creature.*'
That what they're saying". He flaps one wing
over his eyes
and has another.
The old fellow is near to crying.
What can I tell him?
The sad madness
for everything bygone's in his eye.
Names won't touch him.

Young men
are only schoolboys. The old are dry,
and desiccated
or else he'd know them
off by heart. "Then again", he moans,
"the little mott said
the Dail was filled
with fine talkers, but just the once
when I got there
not a man was stirring,
and a fellow I met in Kildare Street
said *"That's all finished.*
Since Mick Collins
met his end there's been none of that.
And Dev's an old one now.
There's nothing
left of the real stuff any more.
All they're after
is drawing their money
and maybe making a small law
once in a season
and writing letters
about the economy of the nation.
Parnell, now,
there was a thinking one,
but the priests put him well out of action"
That's what I'm told!"
And he picks a feather
out of his elbow to draw trees
in the spill on the bar.

What can I answer?
A great sadness is in his eyes,
and his lip trembles.
I could say "Triumph
resolves its clamour and learns Art".
or maybe get him
to read Kinsella,
Kavanagh, Clarke, or perhaps start
him off on Flann O'Brien,
Beckett,
the painters, the actors; but why spoil
a good bitterness,
stop a hunger
feeding its passion to the soul?
Why not listen?
I smile. I listen.
"I was a king", he says, "the once,
and a Ruler of King . . ."
His eye, unfocussed,
burns with the liquor of Romance . . .
"And a poet", he says,
"when poets were fellers
you'd take off your hat to down the street.
And still a poet:
Wait while I tell you
the latest little bit I wrote
on Stephen's Green
as a crow came over . . ."
He clears the phlegm, takes a good sight
on the top corner

beyond the vodka,
rustles his thinking, and comes out
with four Hear-All-Ye's
and seven sighings
of soft rain over the long green hills,
and a number of random
saints and blackbirds
hearing the Monastery bells
as Kathleen passes,
an Old Woman
seeking her bit of turf to put
the warmth under
a broth, while playing
a sad harp for the men shot,
and smiles, waiting.
I say nothing.
He lifts up both his trembling wings
and knocks a table over,
roaring
the holiness of the hearts affections,
the sweet simplicities
of the gael,
the tender-heartedness. Why laugh?
slowly he drinks
the placating porter.
Mystically, he lurches off
and I watch him flapping
albatross-like
down the roadway, gathering speed
as cars skid wildly

into the windows,
the garda dance like they're going mad,
and then with a heave,
bounce, lurch, and sudden
thrust he is up and away, gone
over the roofs—
I'd say heading
West and likely to make Boston
well by morning.
And now, turning
back to what's left of the night's composure,
I pull some lively
and some sour,
compose the poem, construct the future.

THREE DUBLINERS

1. *At a Small Table*

Back to the wall,
the small table
collecting glasses
through slow hours,
his face stiffening
into ideal
withdrawal, lucid
furious peace,

he's stopped recalling
the small urge
swelled to vocation
by chalk hands
cramped with certainty,
stopped feeling
the small terrors
engross his mind

at boys' questions.
Strap! Strap!
That is the way
to drive shame
under, shame it!
Lust strikes
small as an adder
but the flame

42

could roar, roar!
A high blaze
he's fought back!
Greater fear
dissolves the small.
A girl's smile
quivers, damns.
Back to the wall,

he's countered it,
protected, blurred,
need fear nothing.
Some things
are surer than life.
Stone-faced,
back to the wall,
defeat sings.

2. *On the Seashore*

He stands on the beach
in a black suit
and a white shirt
and good shoes,
deriding environment.
He picks
neat shells,
lucid about rejections.

From his turning head
round lenses

heliograph
an eleventh commandment,
regret the tide's
indiscriminate maw,
its loose living,
its soft oaths

under the rock.
He frowns, fumbles,
topples a conch with a stick,
drinks
sombrely from the bottle,
levels
a bland muzzle
at salt words

he won't challenge,
the huge sea
merely parenthesis,
his statement
stubborn in black,
its eyes suns,
its feet cramped
in the good shoes.

3. *By the Grand Canal*

Nothing to say
has his own logic,
meditates
by the slow canal

44

with open waistcoat,
hears larksong,
moves like a mist
across fields,

released, smiling.
Crow nor scarecrow
warn or startle,
nor dark hills
fist with meaning;
his own man,
his words lie
between bark and tree,

a loud silence,
a bright dark.
Thus the heroes
born between
winter and summer
die at the stroke
of paradox
on the edge of water,

between, it may be,
grey houses,
with waistcoats open
and ears filled
with lark stillness,
strange as stone,
not man, not god,
go down smiling.

AN IRISH ALBUM

1. *Renaissance*

Mother of myths, the old wonder,
soft syllabling it in the back room
of a tumbling history; quaint tales
tacked on the coat of Colleen Bawn

draggled through ditches; real speech
brought back alive, alive alive-o,
to strut in Dublin; Ireland free
and it still afther playin' the slave

with a squinty syntax, the bould cratur,
takin' a drop at the soft hands
of the fine lady, and Misther Yeats
bewildered entirely, a grand man

and he talking . . . Book of the People,
people meaning the kicked clown
painting up bruises, the fool nigger
giving himself a fool name,

habit of centuries . . . Curtain UP!
The blackface minstrels, the green fools,
authentic music from bogged harps,
Renaissance standing with proud smile

at the simple sweetness, the wise words
of Kiltartan Workhouse, the damp walls
bloody with spittle, Kathleen, blackface,
coughing her guts through Tara's Halls.

2. *The Apple*

Drogheda grey in a grey wind,
the streets empty, I play pilgrim
across to the church to find fruit
of the long rotten tree of Tyburn.

Small on the altar, a yellow apple
wrinkled and shiny, Blessed Plunkett's
head rests, a bland reminder
of kicking crowds, another martyr

good for the books, but old, cold,
the golden head, like the gold bird,
remote in artifice. Who'll pretend
grief for a Phoenix burned out,

a symbol withered? The grey winds
course through Drogheda's grey dust,
breathless with futures. The head sits
emptied and still. The winds pass

Spenser's century, Cromwell's, Pitt's,
but Holy Ireland, History galloping
by her, stumbled, paused, picked
up the apple, is still running.

3. *Ditch Logic*

Under a Kerry hedge, light shaking
holy emblems of dogrose, briar,
and raindrop silver, the gaunt Father
spelled out Suffering, every letter

another footfall to stop the breath
at God's Wisdom who kept such holy
servitude for the pure Irish,
surely a chosen and flailed people

blessed by revilings and persecutions,
children to sweetly cry Hail Mary
under the blackbird, humble knees
on burned earth at the curlew's cry

through mist drifting. I walk Ireland
listening, suffering the same mists
threaded by music, the same words
but from a plump and different priest

with a house of statues, a cord of candles,
a bloody heart on the great door:
The poor are always with us, blessed:
God is opposed to Medicare.

4.   *The Return of Casement*

Casement returns. Already stories
of miraculous preservation
trouble the papers; lime could not
rot, nor clay sour his sweet bones.

This I believe, for a man should
accept whatever surpasses fact
with purest vision. Why doubt?
Practice in faith becomes perfect

blinding clarity, all Truth
a lake of mirrors improving light
with dear refraction. As for Casement:
whether or not the worm and rot

gouged or the lime burned, doesn't matter.
Reverence transforms its every use,
and better this tyrant-hating gentle
knight than the usual crouched recluse.

5.   *Geasa*
Forbidden drink, the arms of women
about his neck, and lewd words,
Murphy, no less than Conaire trapped
by rule of the long-plumed King of Birds,

awaits fury, a great thirst
black in his throat, a dry mouth
aching for softness, a small sad
blasphemy whistling in his breath

as darkness nears and the wild horde
of hound-voiced geese on northward wings
announces destiny, priests gathering
watchful as crows for the last things.

6.   *Fallguy of the Western World*
I take up my pen . . . (pauses, scratches,
 fumbles a bottle from a cupboard . . .)
Ancient Ireland . . . (eyes glazing,
gives more Powers to his elbow) . . .

Scholars and Saints . . . (abandons, crumples,
hats head, macs back, is off out
to the Pearl Bar, car radio
jiving sweetly among grey streets

young ankles skip and bottoms bobble . . .
corks on a dangerous tide rising;
three Hail Marys against that
and all lechery! Later, easing

primal flux up a black alley,
steaming the wall, in a thin voice) . . .
Take me home . . . Kathleen . . . poor bloody
(sobbing) *get of the sad Irish* . . .

THE RETURN OF SUIBHNE

It was on a summer's evening.
I was listening
to my own head making music
from chinking glass
and regretting I couldn't whistle
when Mad Suibhne
stalked into the bar,
in feathers from head to ass,

chirruping like a sailor.
I recognized him
immediately
from the rattle of his lung
and the one eye round as a marble.
He called the curate
something monstrous
and roared for another one

to which he applied the eye,
and its golden whirlpool
whistled back as he stared.
He husked: "I see
the fierce potato
pushing its milk-white fingers
into the womb of the world,
destroying pity.

This is the mandrake monster!
When it screamed,
tugged from the blackened earth
by a wicked hound
seven centuries died
and a people vanished
into the stench of corruption,
holding hands

hopelessly up to the light;
this was the emblem
snug in the pocket of lust
when Circe winked
the voyagers into swine,
the deadly message
stitching up the lips
of rhetorical flesh.

"This", he rasped, "is the god!"
And from the pocket
of his heron-ribbed flank
he pulled a withered
spud with the face of a woman.
"Shan Van Vocht",
he muttered, "and tinker Houlihan's
wrinkled daughter,

Ireland, Ireland, Ireland!"
I crossed my fingers,
my legs, and myself very quickly
and, spilling slightly,

leaned through a hover of hiccups
to answer back
in tones of unreasonable reason,
but he had sidled

off through the gap in logic
and was seated
hunched as a crow
at the far end of the bar,
pouring a little hot water.
I followed, lurching
on account of uncrossing my legs,
but had not got far

when weakness overtook me
with sudden abandon
of speech and the use of my knees.
He gave a chirp
of gloomy satisfaction,
folded his wings
about his enormous belly
and fell asleep

like a child on the breast of its mother.
I mouthed for words
but nothing came out but a whistle.
I'd meant to claim
Tradition, History, Scholarship,
Beauty, Religion,
but slowly his figure,
the colour of storm-swept stone,

began to alter and blur
till all remaining
was a shimmer of mist,
an empty glass,
and a leather-brown wrinkled potato.
I have the potato
here on the end of my watch-chain,
just in case . . .

BEN BULBEN REVISITED

"Irish Poets, learn your trade"
he told us. Must we then think back
"on other days", again fashion
history into a rhetoric?

I scout that. Blake said
"Drive your cart and plow over
the bones of the dead." "Expect
poison from the standing water."

"Irish Poets remake the past."
I think is better. Trouble
the dreams of those persistent ghosts
guttering the stiff candle.

Mimic the mind that found Truth
out, and held it against odds,
the achieved reverence, the hard won
simplicity, not the dead word.

Rewrite History twice written,
both times for a blind cause;
doubt the heroes; expose the saints;
canonise the indifferent house.

Search out the centre. Speak from
knowledge of all that make speech,
hub not circumference. Spend words
with the security of the rich.

Learn ceremony; move stiff
brocades easy as moving water;
watch rivers; measure style
against the fluidities of the lover.

Listen. Listen. A poem's guile
is knowledge of silence, a poem's truth
the twist of a syllable. Hear in
the stamp of armies the dragging foot.

Praise that step, and reverence all
individual vision; see
mass rhythm break at the lame god's
indomitable artistry.